My Animal Alphabet
Paintings and Poems

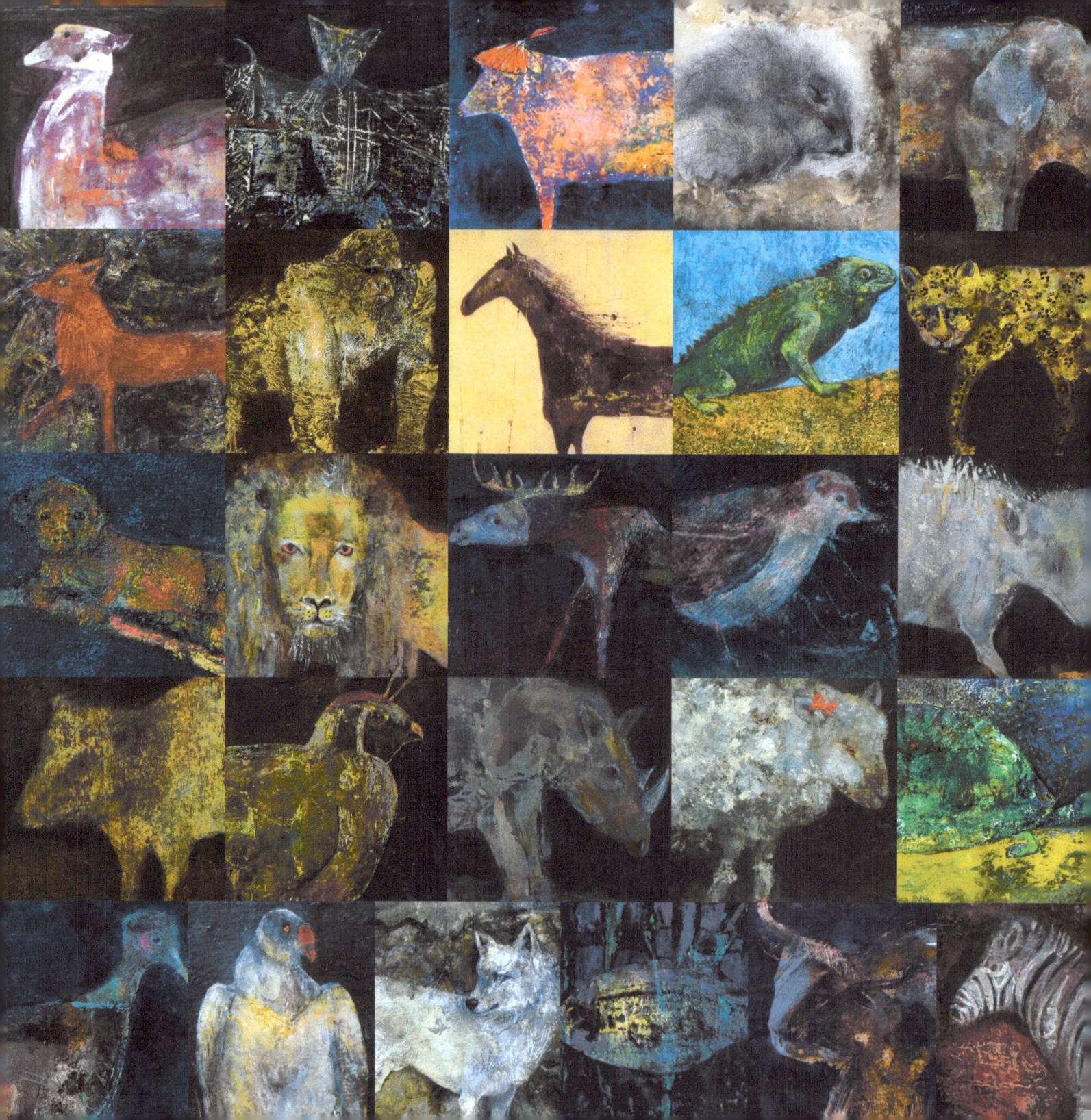

My Animal Alphabet
Paintings and Poems

by

Linda Mia Turkel

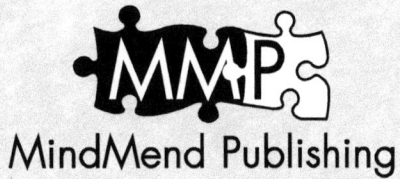

MindMend Publishing

Published in 2014 by MindMend Publishing Co., New York, NY

Printed in the United States of America on acid free paper.

Library of Congress Control Number: 2014954358

Cataloging Data:

Turkel, Linda Mia. My Animal Alphabet: Paintings and Poems / Linda Mia Turkel.

1. Art : Subjects & Themes - Plants & Animals.
2. Poetry / Subjects & Themes / Nature.
3. Education : Non-Formal Education.

ISBN-13: 978-0-9848700-9-7 (soft cover)

ISBN-13: 978-1-942431-00-8 (hard cover)

Book design, editing, and illustrations - by MindMendMedia, Inc. @ MindMendMedia.com

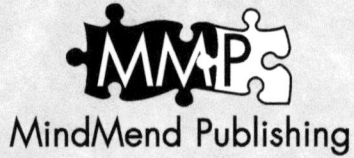

MindMend Publishing

To my husband,
Henry,

To my sons,
Max, Sam, Harry, Jack,

To my granddaughters,
Esther, Sam, Mira,

with love

Introduction

I thought that I would write in this introduction something about why animals are so important to me, and why, before I created this alphabet, they seemed to appear in so much of my art. Once I began to try to explain this, I realized that it is very complex, and that the subject of people (especially children) and their relationship to animals would be more appropriate in a longer essay. I also hadn't really thought it through, I think, because rendering images of animals can replace the need to explain the feelings.

I thought of how various animals can represent different aspects of human feeling and behavior, and may therefore be symbols of how we feel. It even may be safer to experience feelings when they are expressed through animals. In my work many animals can be found.

Well, one day, my friend Brigid said to me, "why don't you do an animal alphabet?"

Although the idea intrigued me, I thought, "I don't really have an animal for each letter. I have an awful lot of cats, and many of my animals don't exist in the real world."

But what was so alluring about this suggestion was the notion of using the alphabet as a framework for painting these animals. The alphabet is one of the constants in our life that we don't think about that much, except of course when we're very young and first learning it. It is the beginning of reading, and on its own, makes a very nice song:

"A-B-C-D-E-F-G……………………………………………………….."

So I went about gathering animals, using the ones I had already done, and adding new ones as I journeyed through the alphabet. I found it interesting and challenging to find an animal for each letter – a "real" animal. I already had many "invented" creatures that seemed to spring from my imagination, but I decided that the rules would be that each animal would come from the real world, (although possibly impressionistic) and that I would not represent any species more than once, if possible.

I consulted the encyclopedia a lot. Hence, kinkajou, upland plover, and X-ray fish. This was fun.

I finished my alphabet after about six months and I felt good about it. And then my husband Henry said, "why don't you now write a little poem about each animal?"

"What??????" I had just spent such a long time with these animals and that was my first response to Henry's suggestion, "what????????????"

But I do like making up rhymes and this idea wouldn't leave my head. So I spent the next three months writing little verses for each animal. The only way I could achieve a good meter was by walking, which suited me fine. So this I did. I walked and walked through the alphabet with my animals, and here they are.

Alpaca

The alpaca's like a llama,

Not so big and somewhat calma.

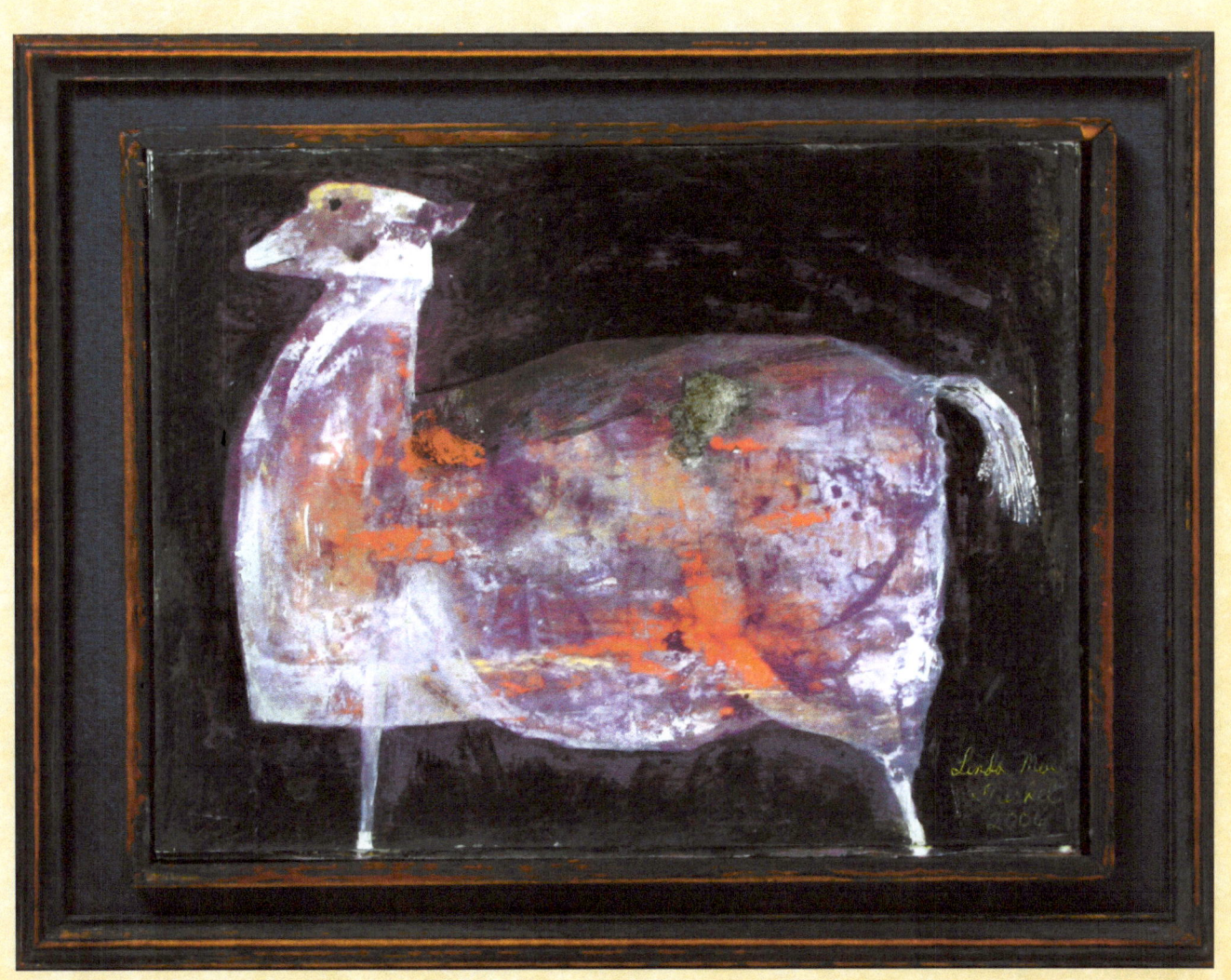

Bat

This odd and lovely creature

That you see in the night sky,

She sleeps by day and

She's the only mammal that can fly.

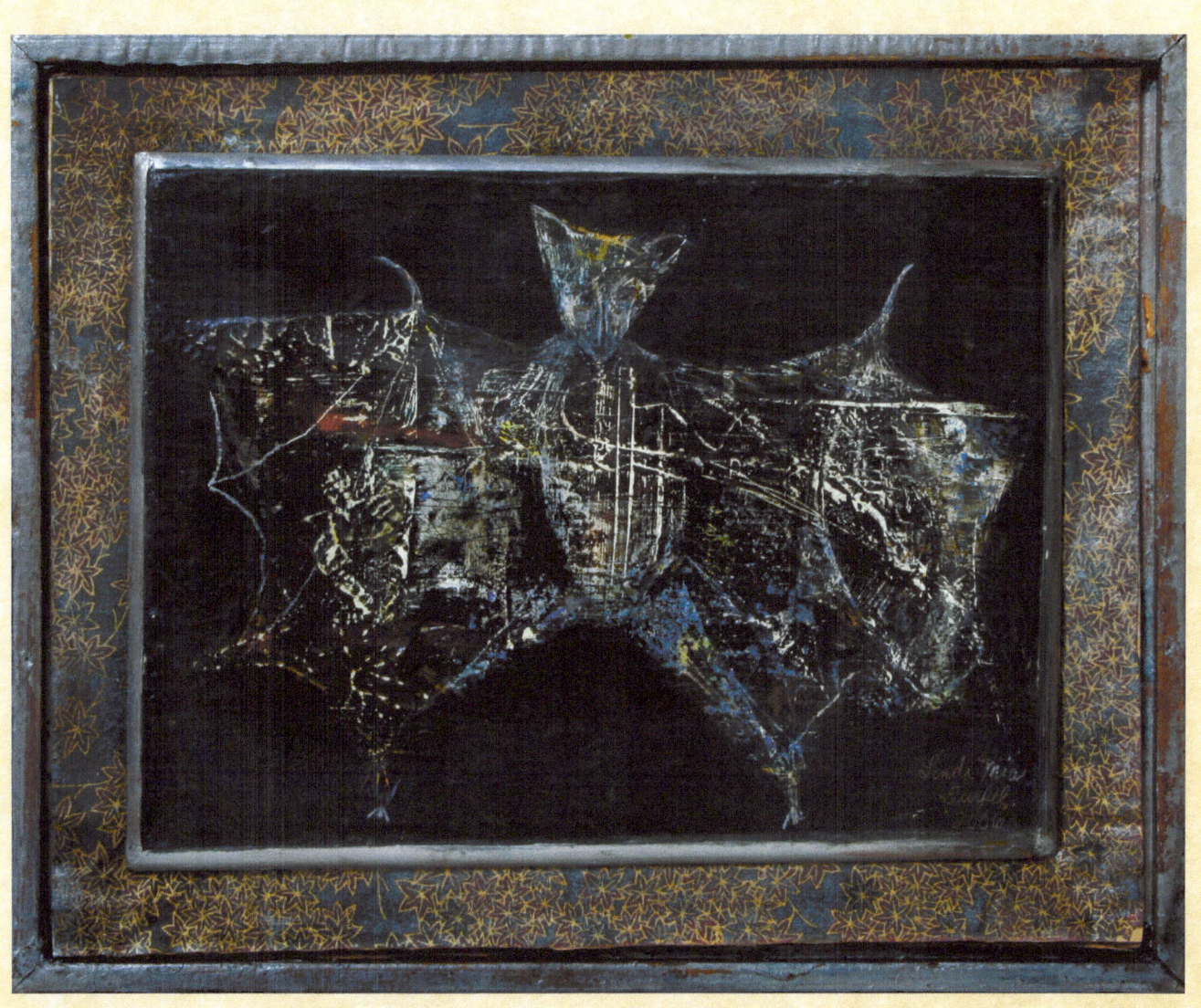

Cow

A lady wears a hat and so

I gave one to this cow-

For I was hoping that it might

Appeal to her somehow.

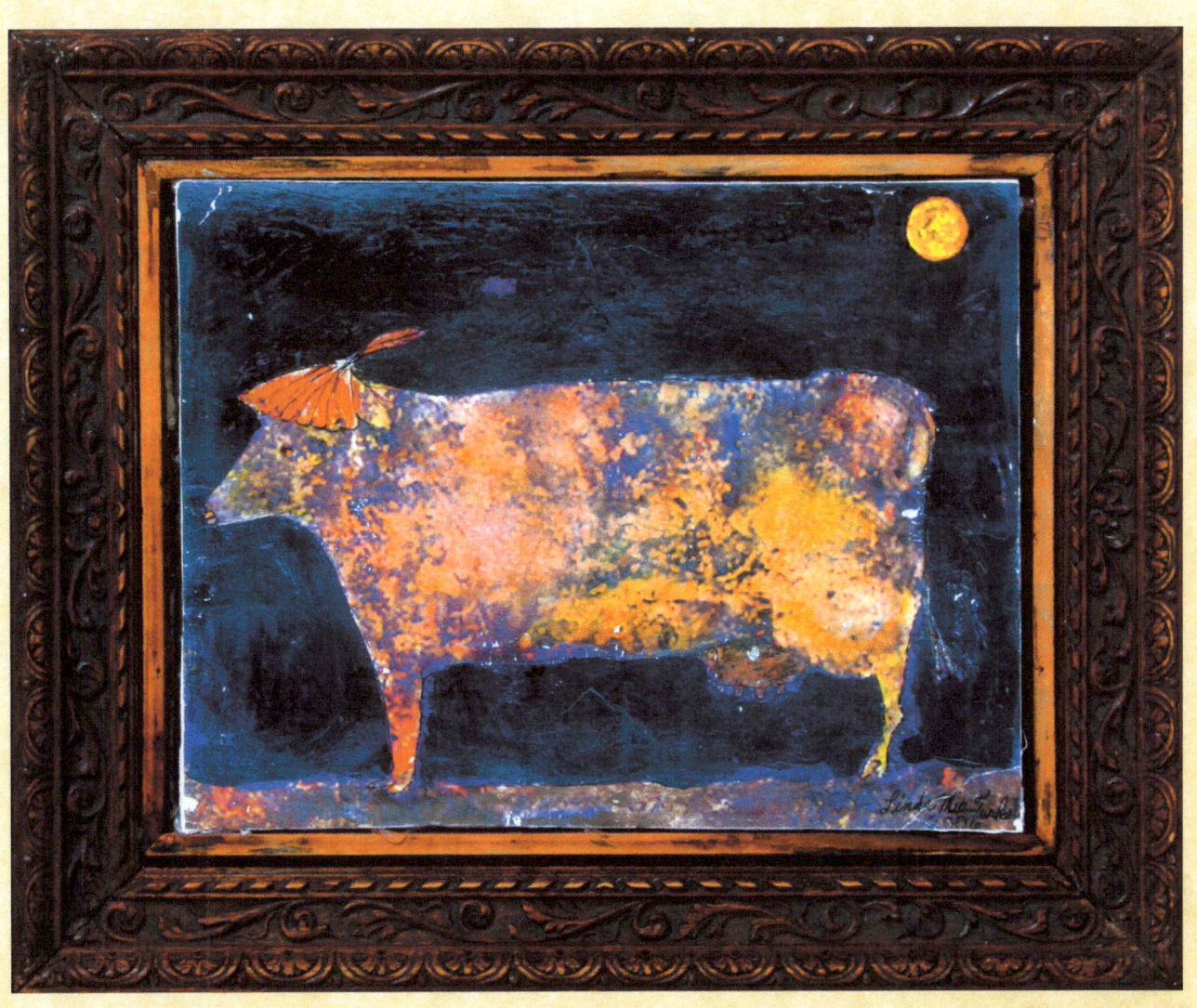

Dormouse

This dormouse doesn't like the cold.

He shuns the winter's sting.

He made a nest inside this page –

I'll keep him 'till the spring.

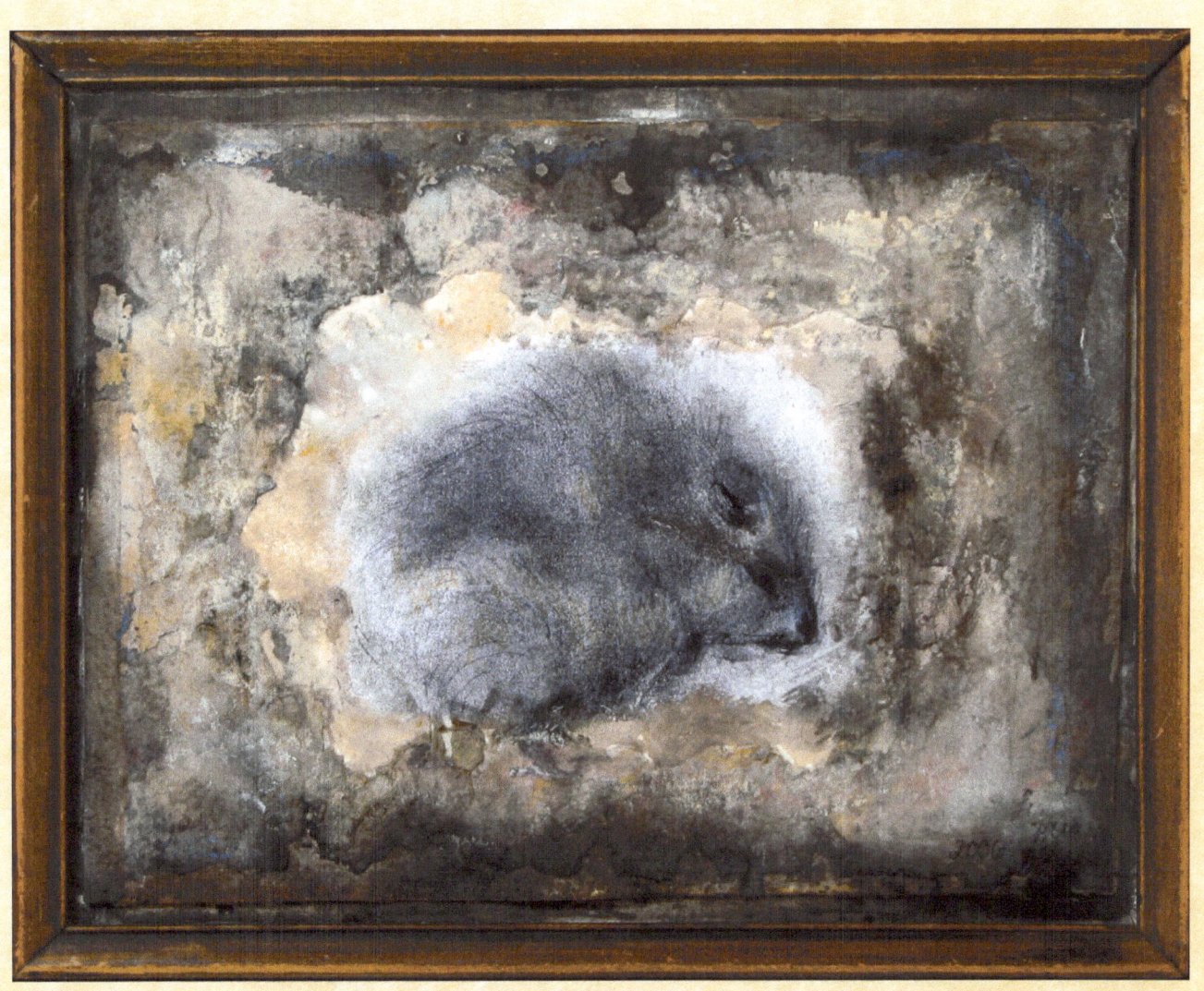

Elephant

The elephant is elegant,

And this I do contend;

No other animal looks so much

Alike at either end.

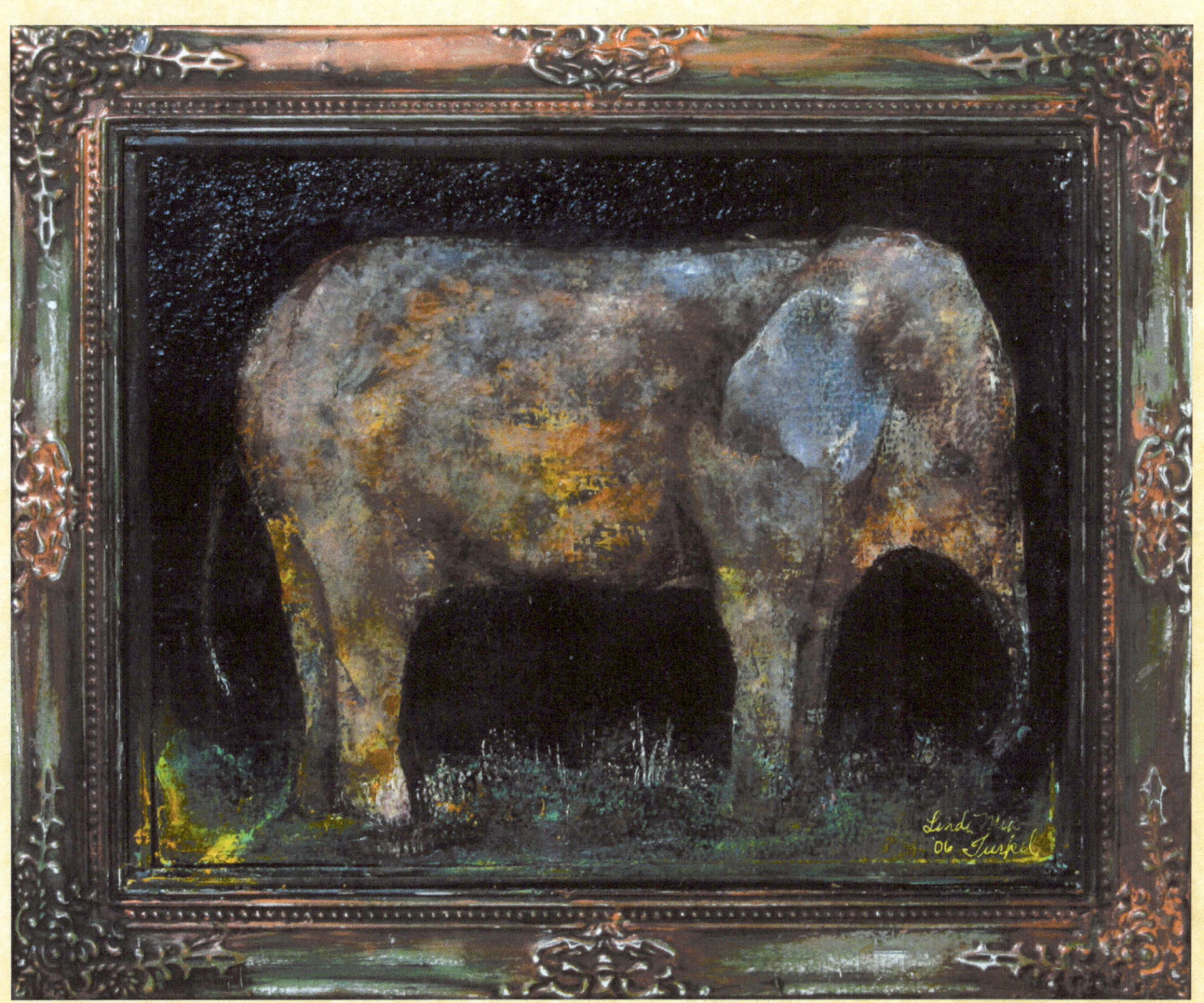

Fox

This fox is awfully busy.

He's both predator and prey.

The rabbit he runs after –

From the hound he runs away.

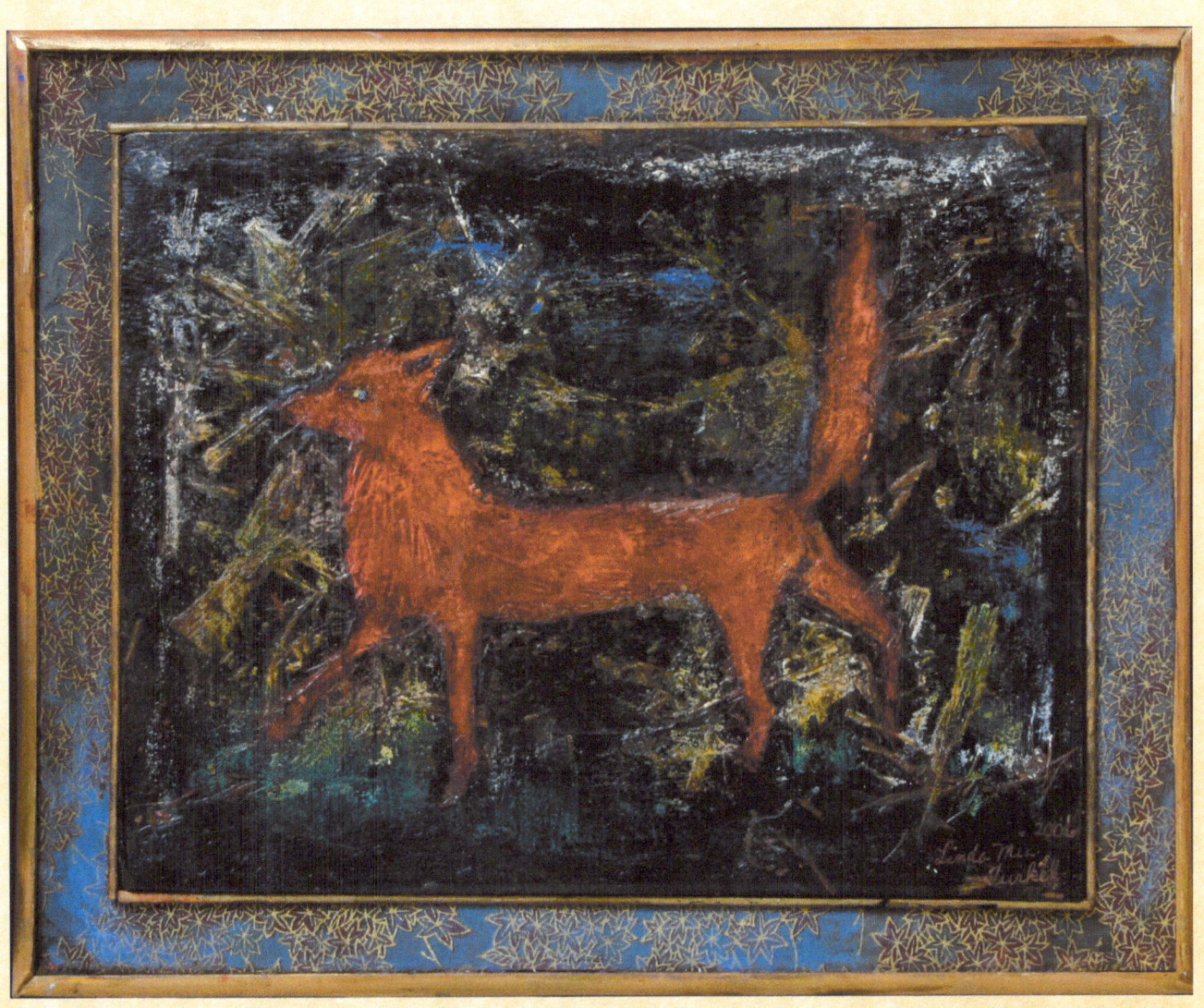

Gorilla

As I wandered through my mind

Hoping an image would unfold,

I came across a large gorilla,

With a dark sad face of gold.

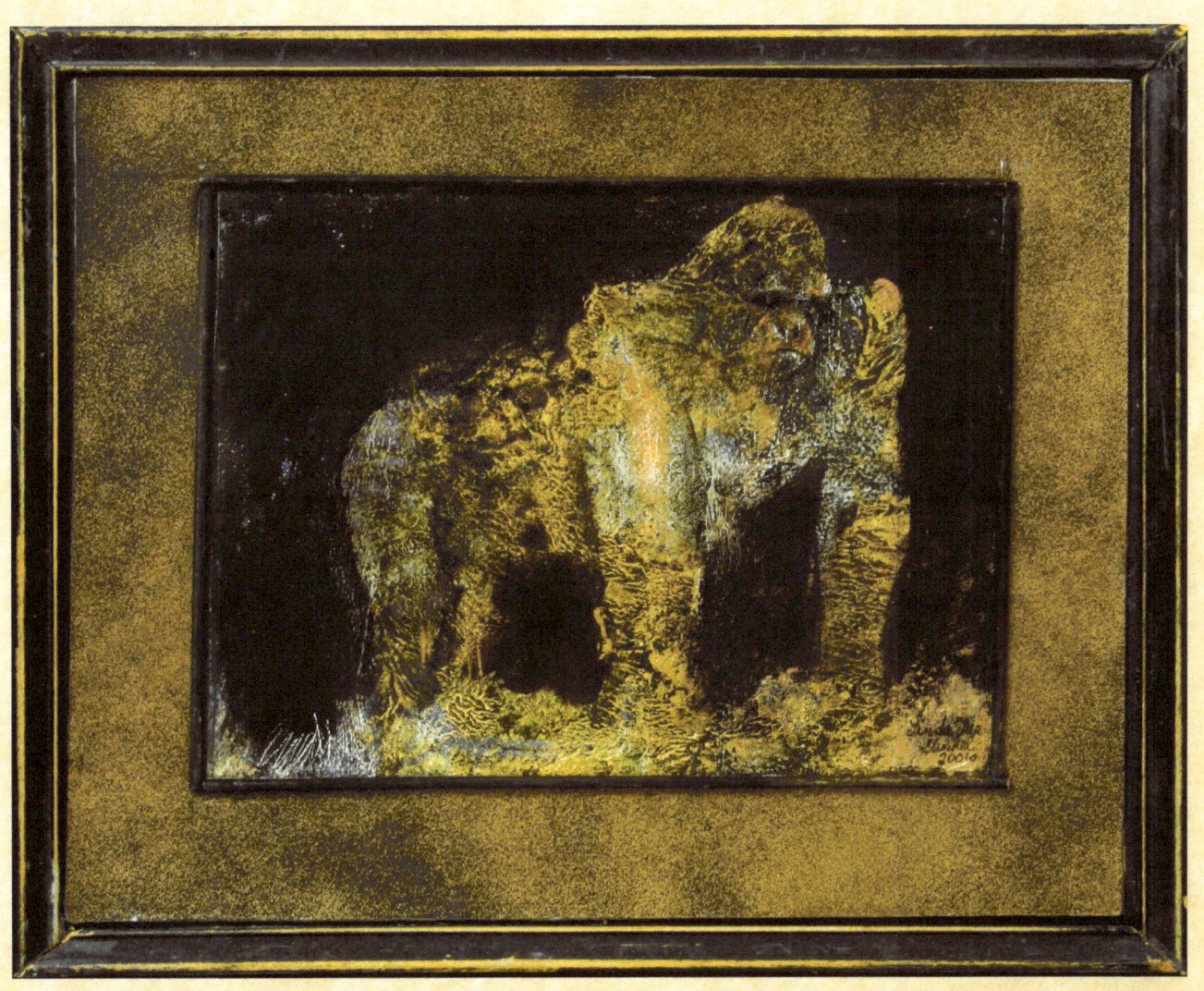

Horse

This horse is a bronze beauty,

As he prances all around.

He is just like a dancer,

His feet barely touch the ground.

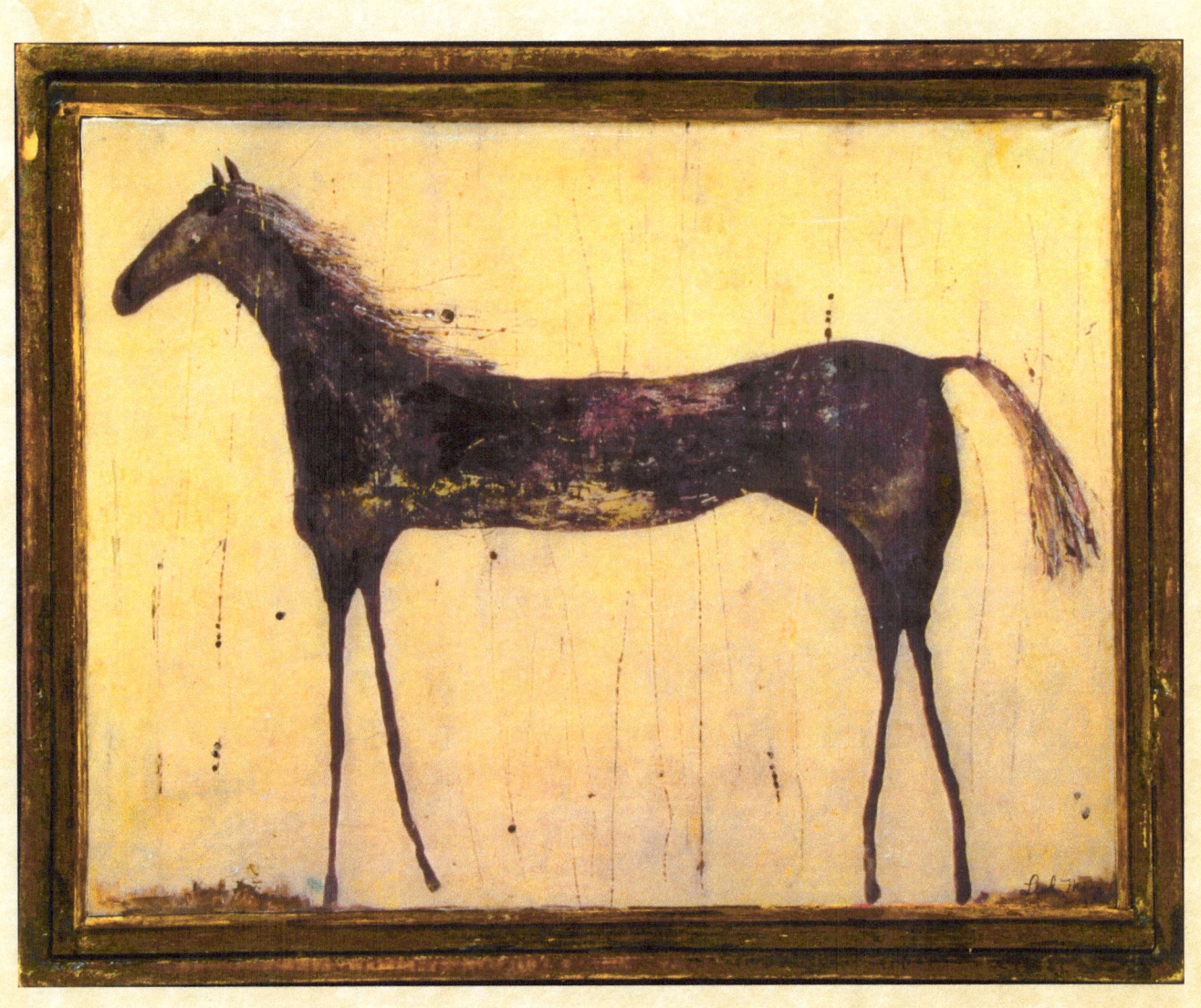

Iguana

I painted this iguana.

What he waits for I don't know.

I think he is just sunning.

When he warms up off he'll go.

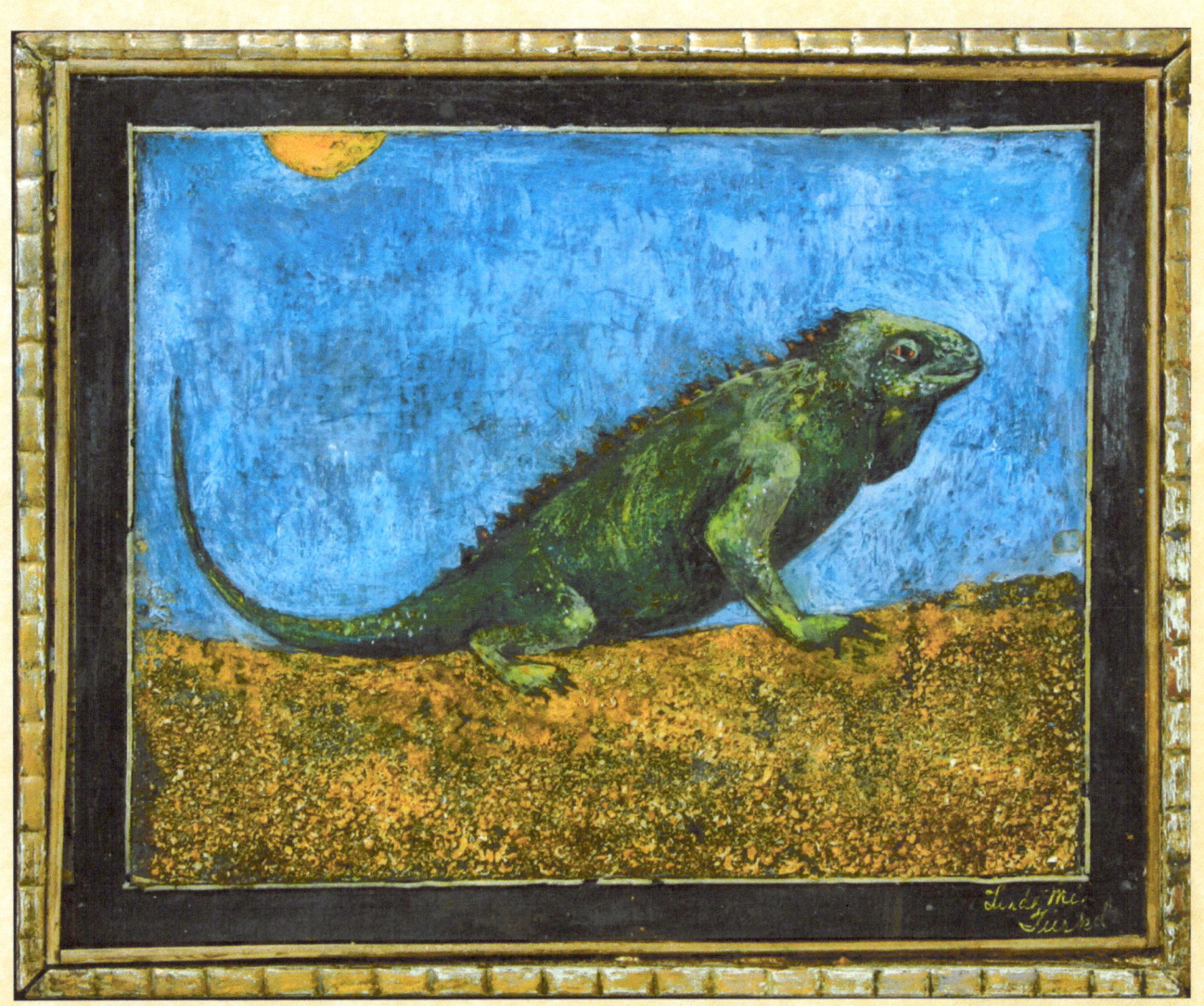

Jaguar

A thousand blooms of black and gold

Light up a jaguar's coat.

His eyes shine out like emeralds

As he eats a mountain goat.

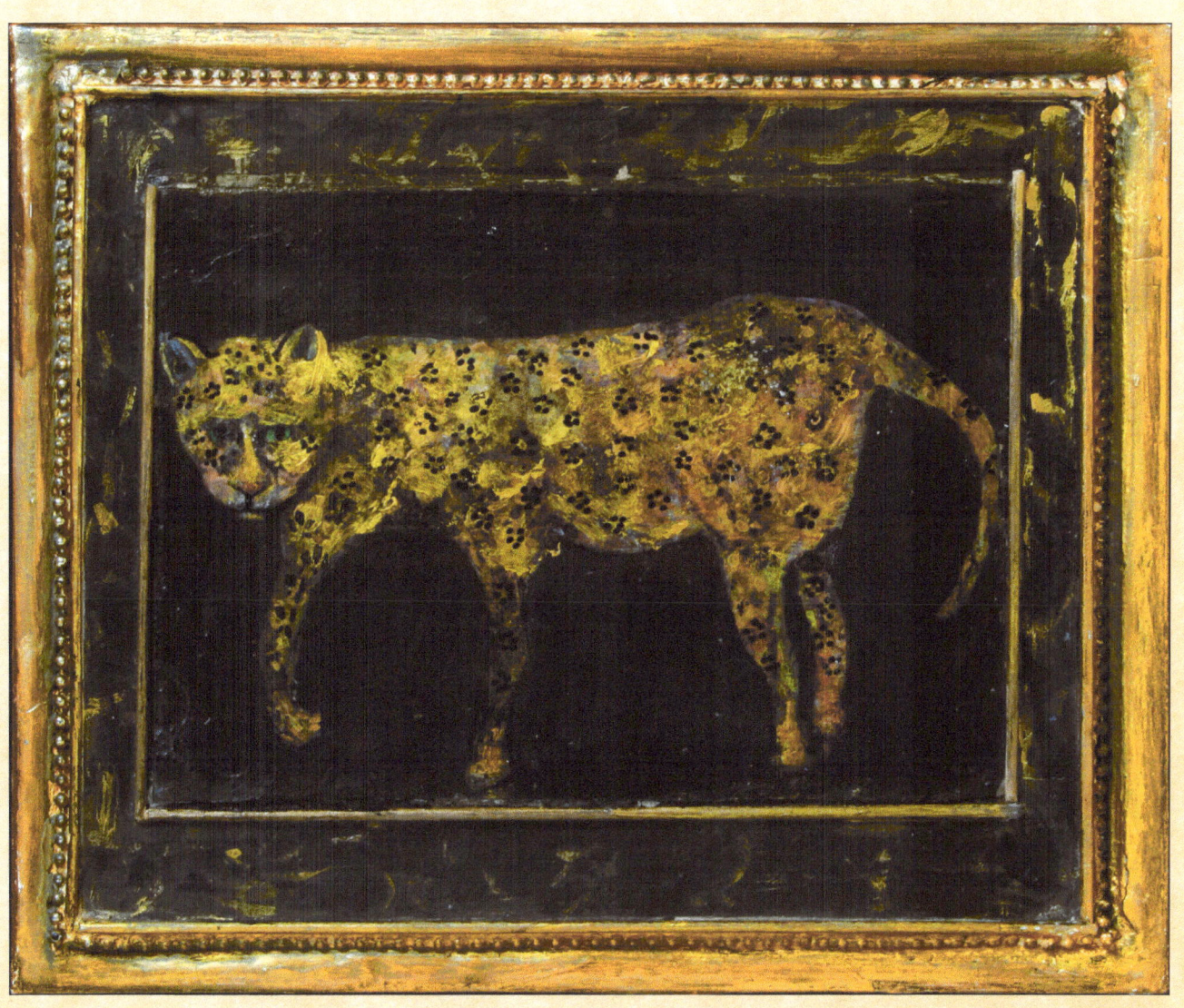

Kinkajou

The kinkajou, he lives in trees

Where he hangs upside down.

His name sounds something like a sneeze

His coat is tannish brown.

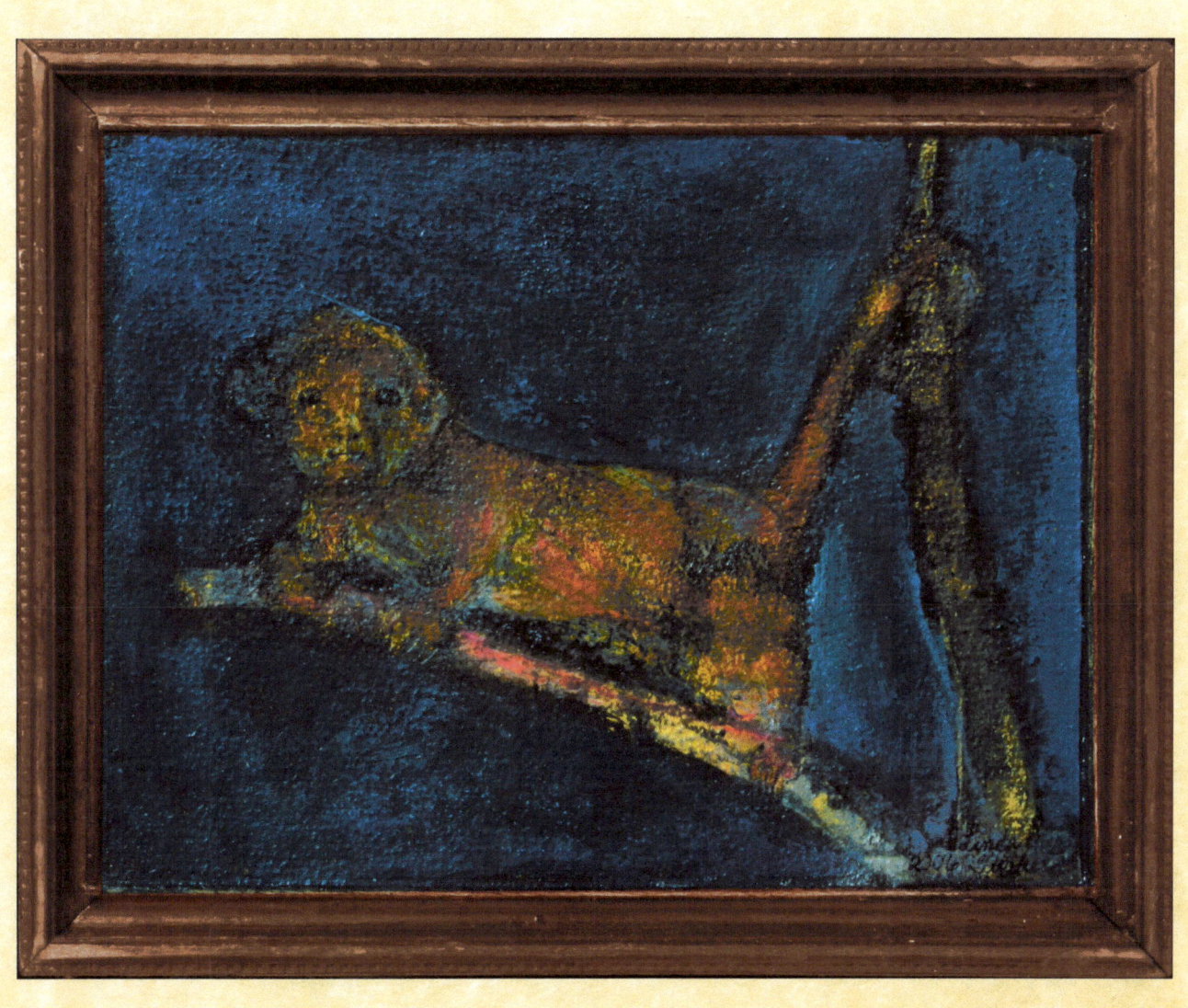

Lion

This lion's old and haggard,

But his mane is still quite glorious.

And when he can remember,

He lets go a sound uproarious.

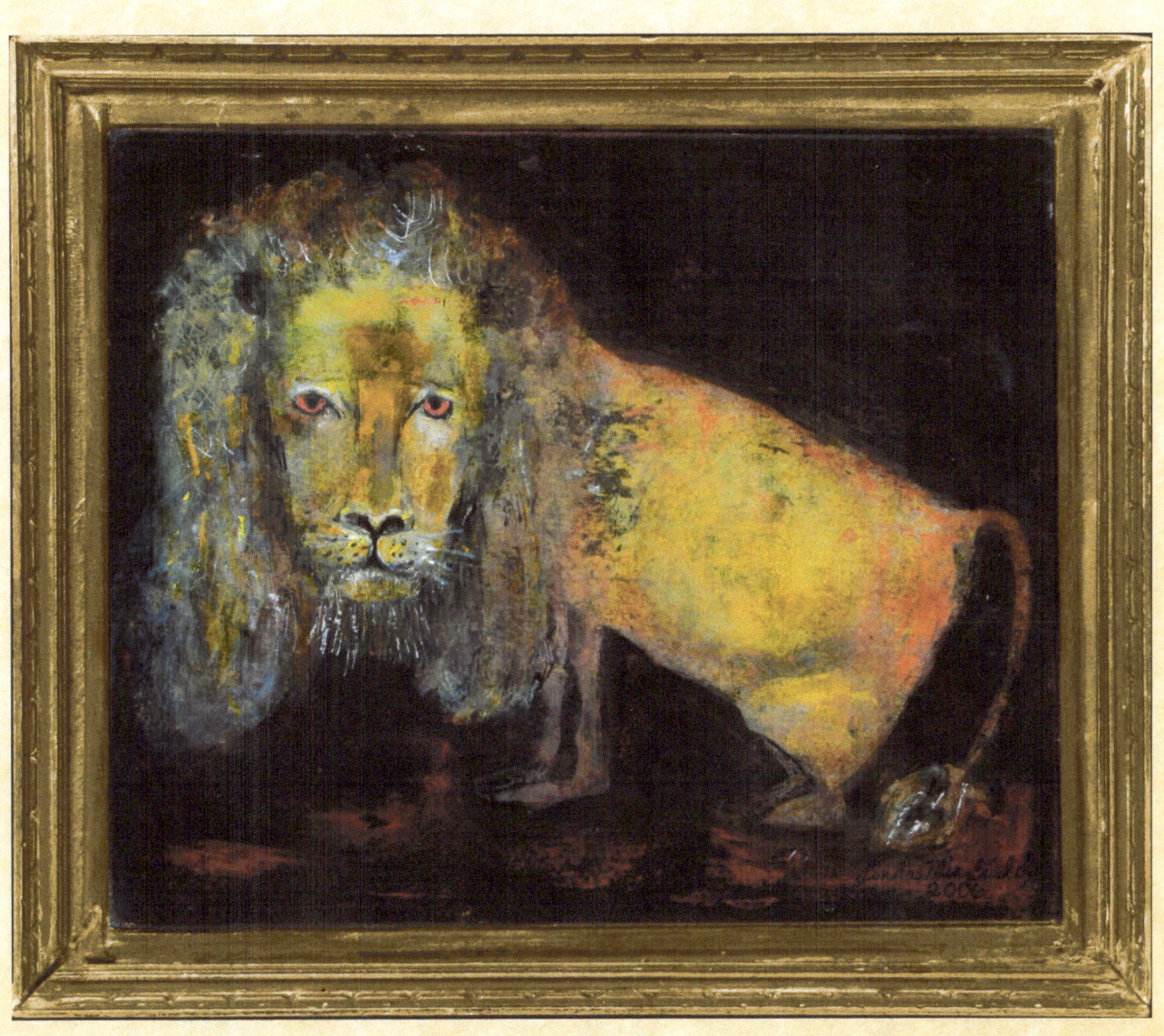

Moose

I met a moose on Main Street

In the middle of the morn.

This moose was most momentous,

And the huge span of his horn

Impressed me.

So I said to him:

"When next will you be here?"

He answered:

"I'm not certain, but I don't think 'till next year."

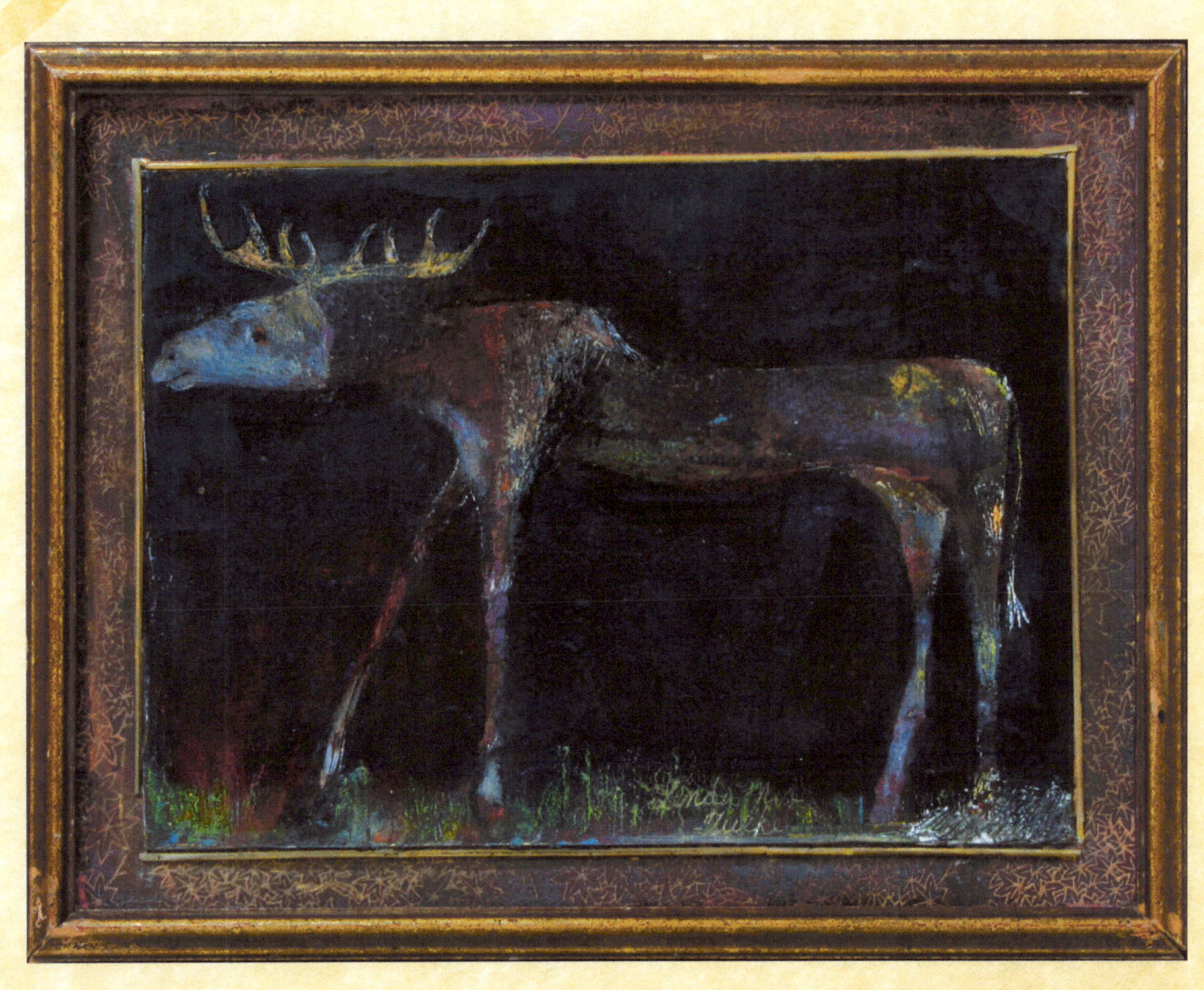

Nightingale

I was thinking of the nightingale

Walking near my mother's home

Hoping that my muse would come

And send to me a poem.

But instead I tripped and fell

Upon this rocky road.

So I refer you to John Keats –

Please read his perfect ode.

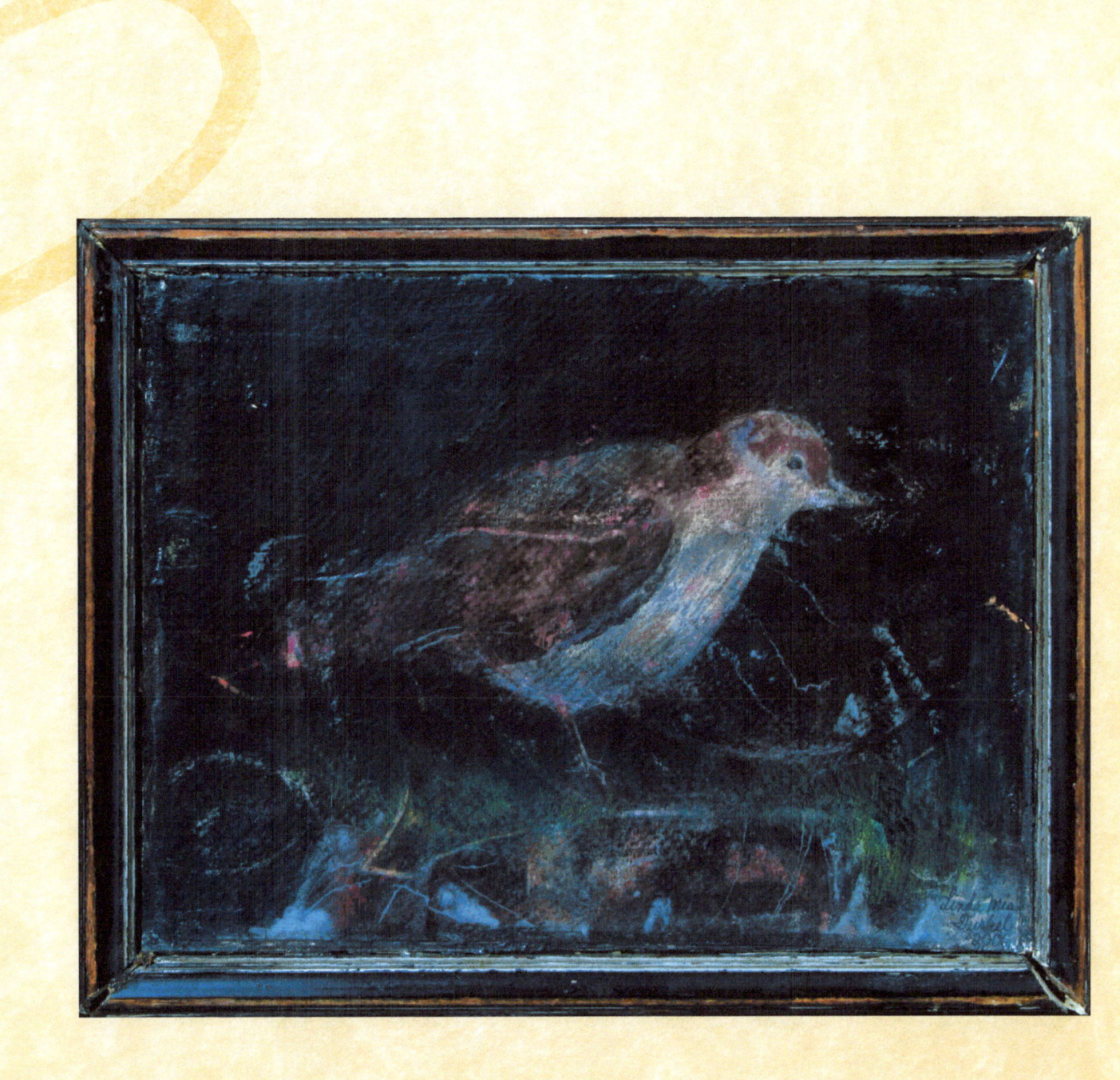

Opossum

The opossum has a good trick:

He can't run fast; instead,

When pursued by a predator,

He just stops and plays dead.

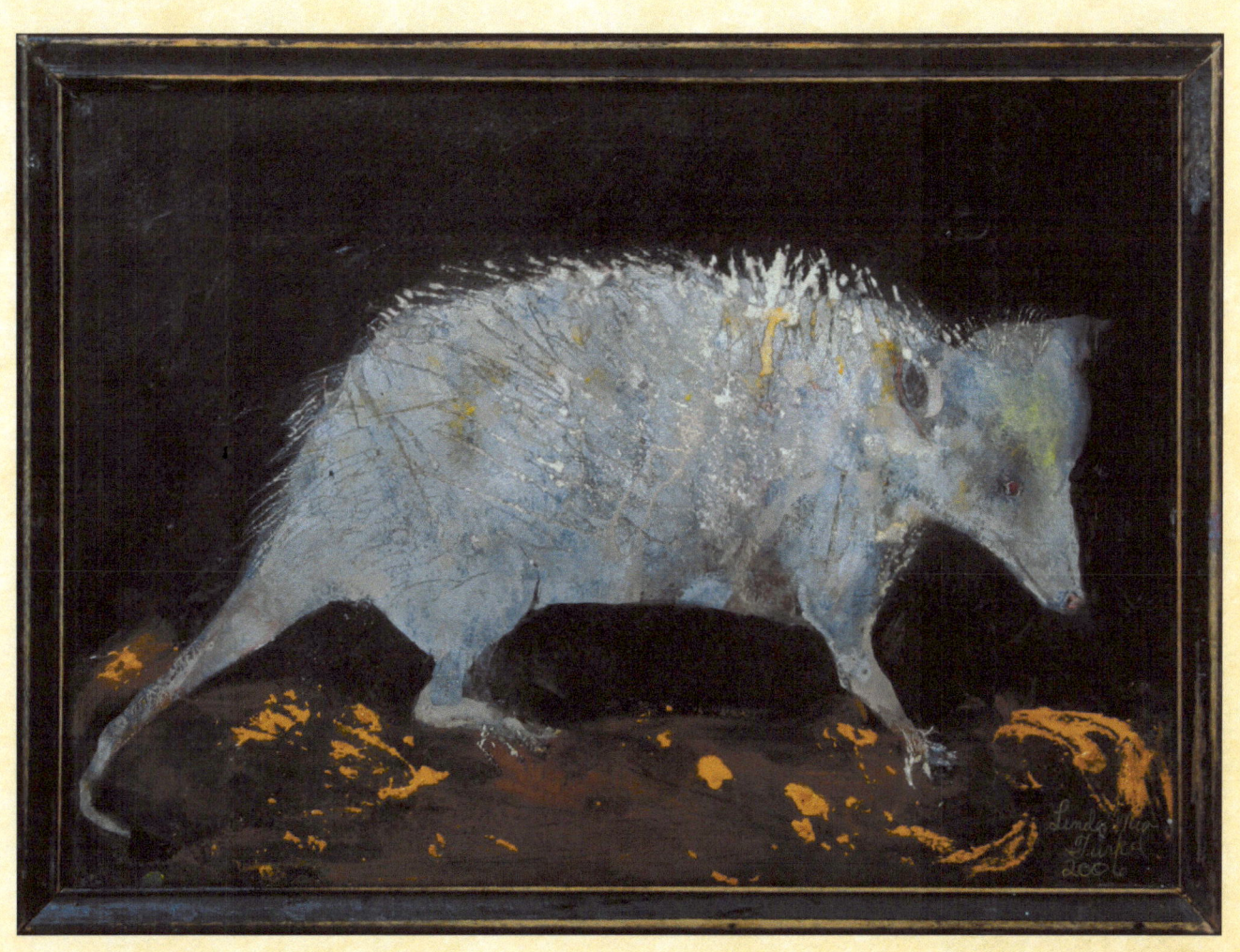

Peccary

The peccary is hog like

With a musk sac on his back.

He's timid, but when frightened –

With a foul smell – will attack.

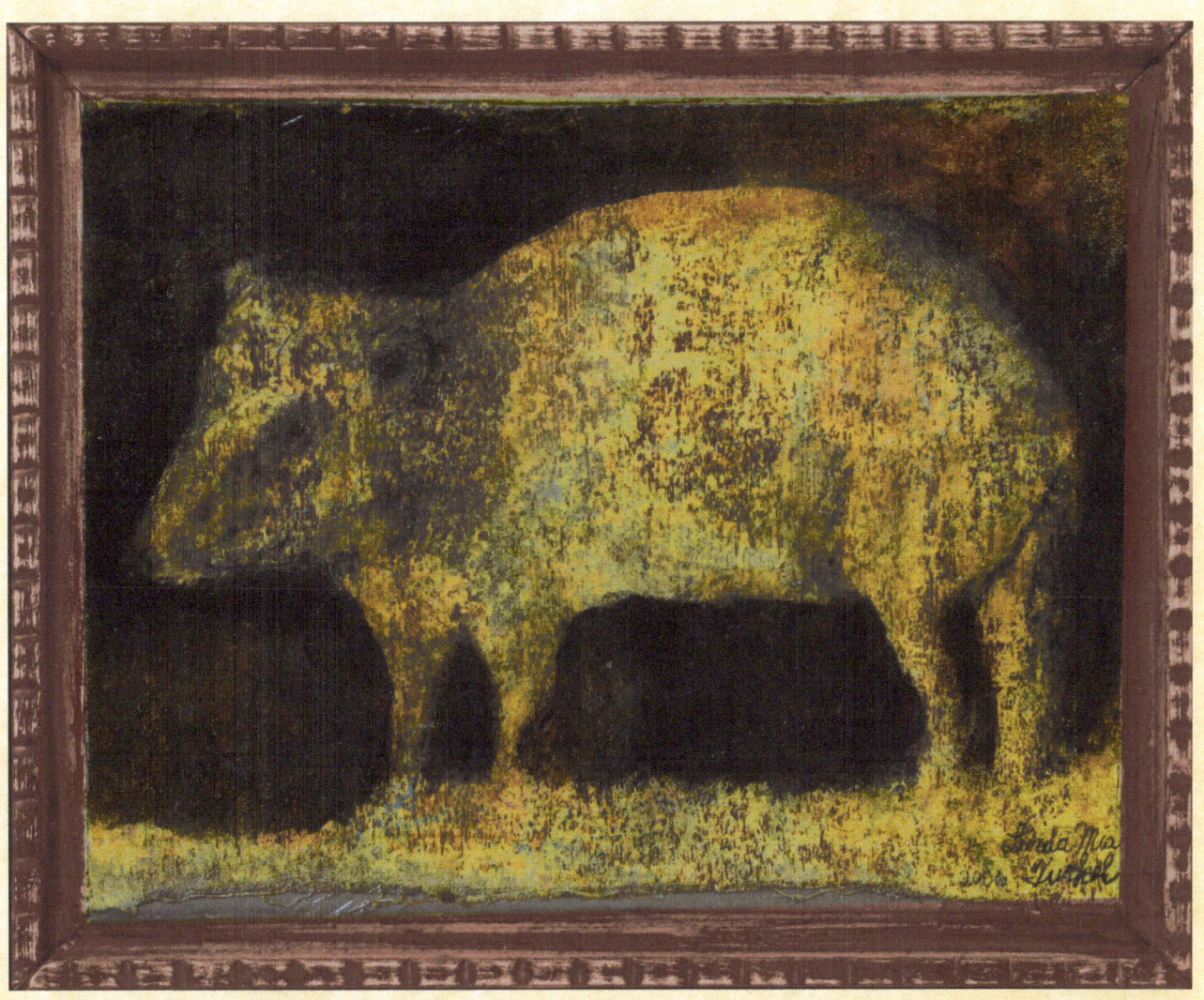

Quail

Hail, Sir Quail – may I avail

Of you to pose for me?

Your plumed hat, your courtly strut –

You are a prince to see.

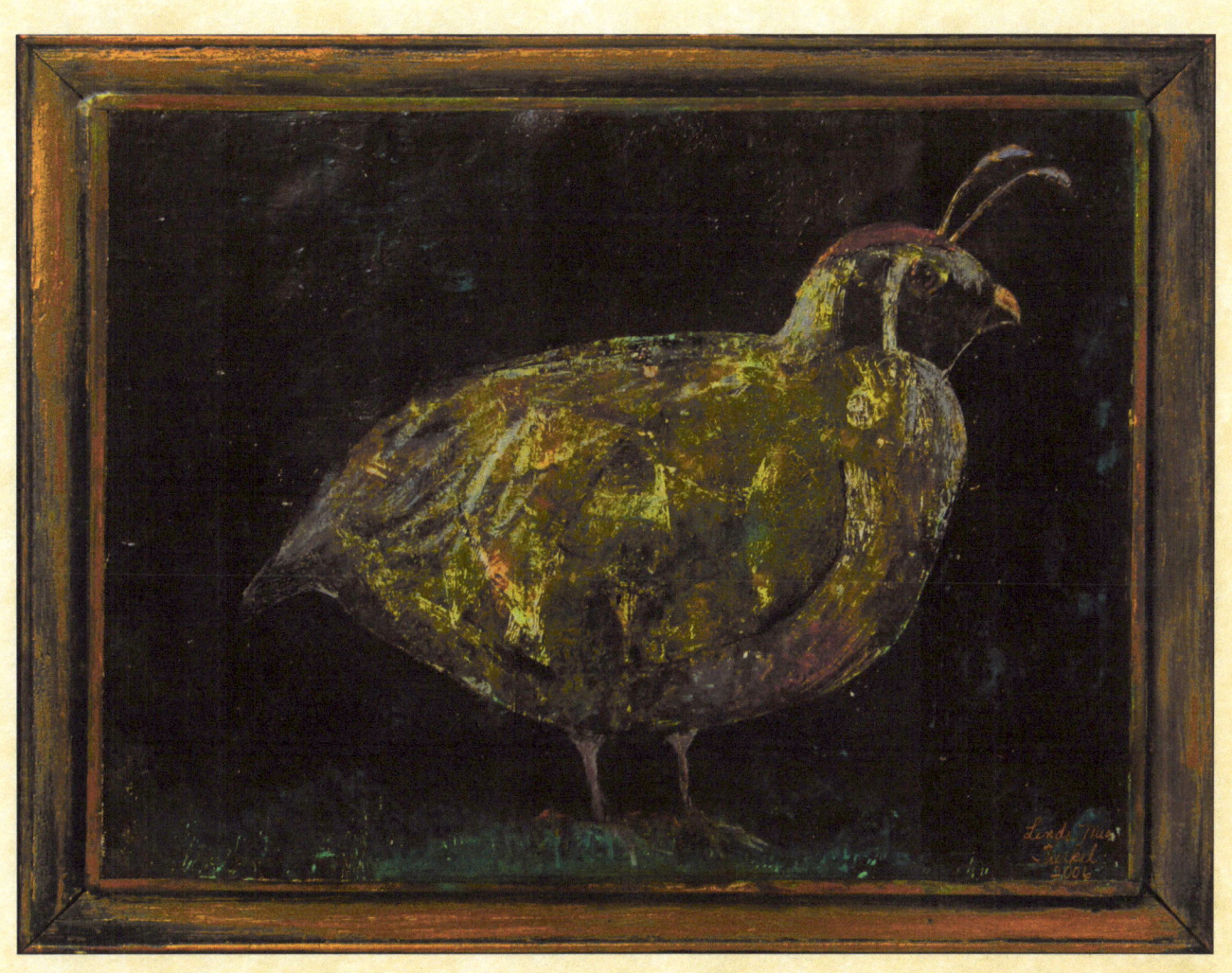

Rhinoceros

Behold the great rhinoceros,

He can weigh two tons.

He lumbers when he walks –

But watch out when he runs.

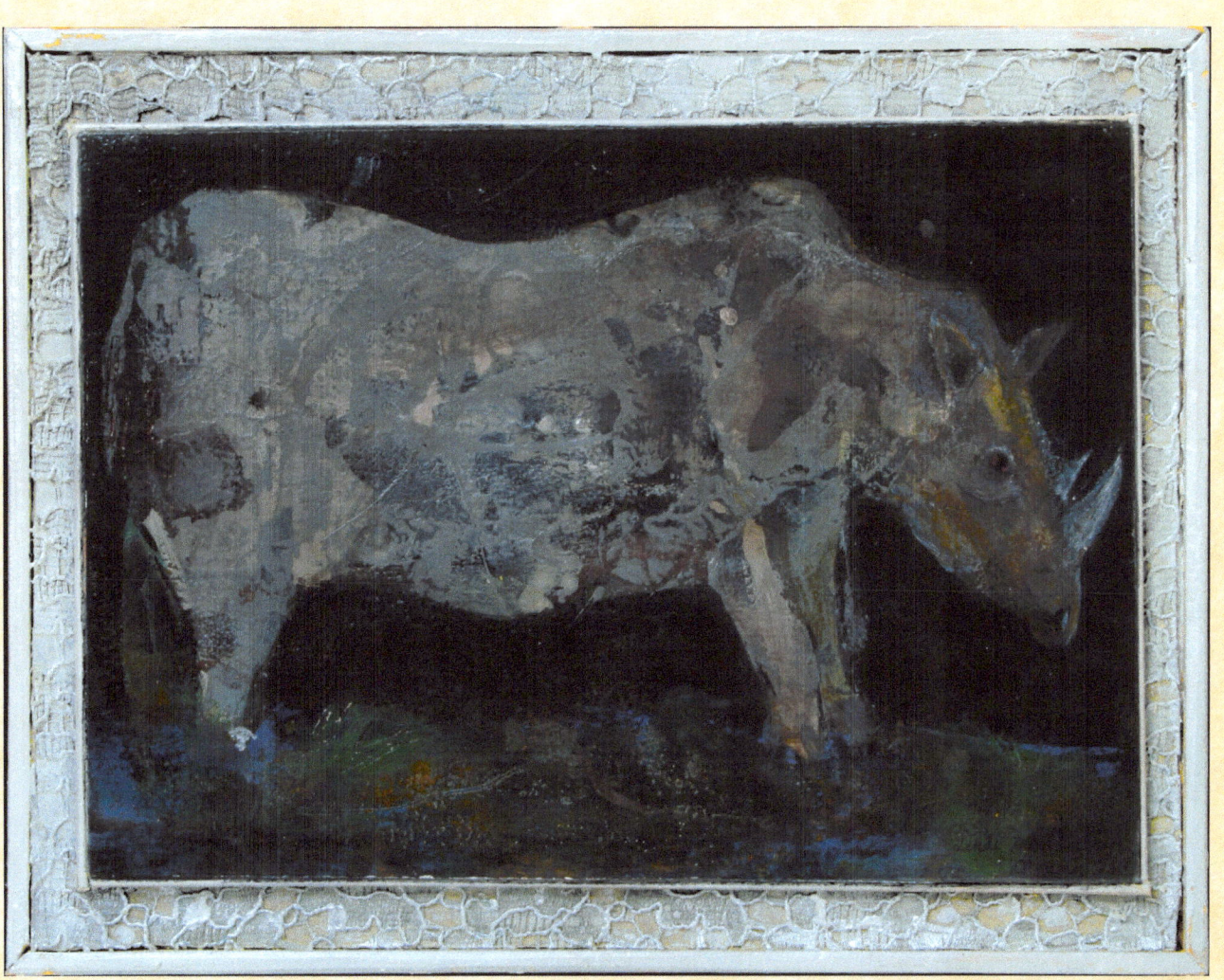

Sheep

The sheep will keep her fleece

Until the summer when she's shorn.

Then her wool will make a coat,

And on another's back be worn.

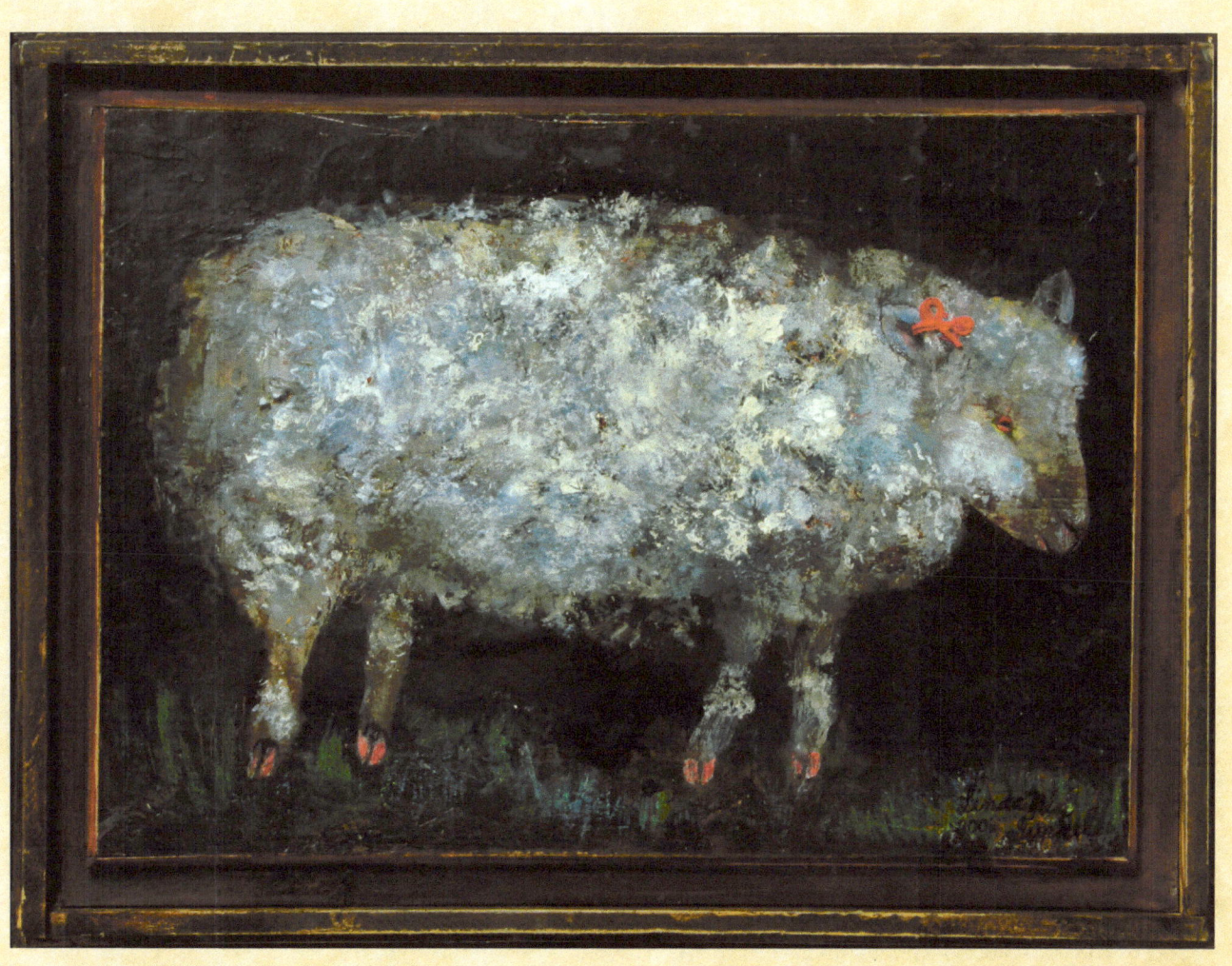

Turtle

A house of green tiles

Shelters this turtle.

It's inhabited by him alone.

And though such a top heavy load

Seems a burden – he lives so long,

His life span's not known.

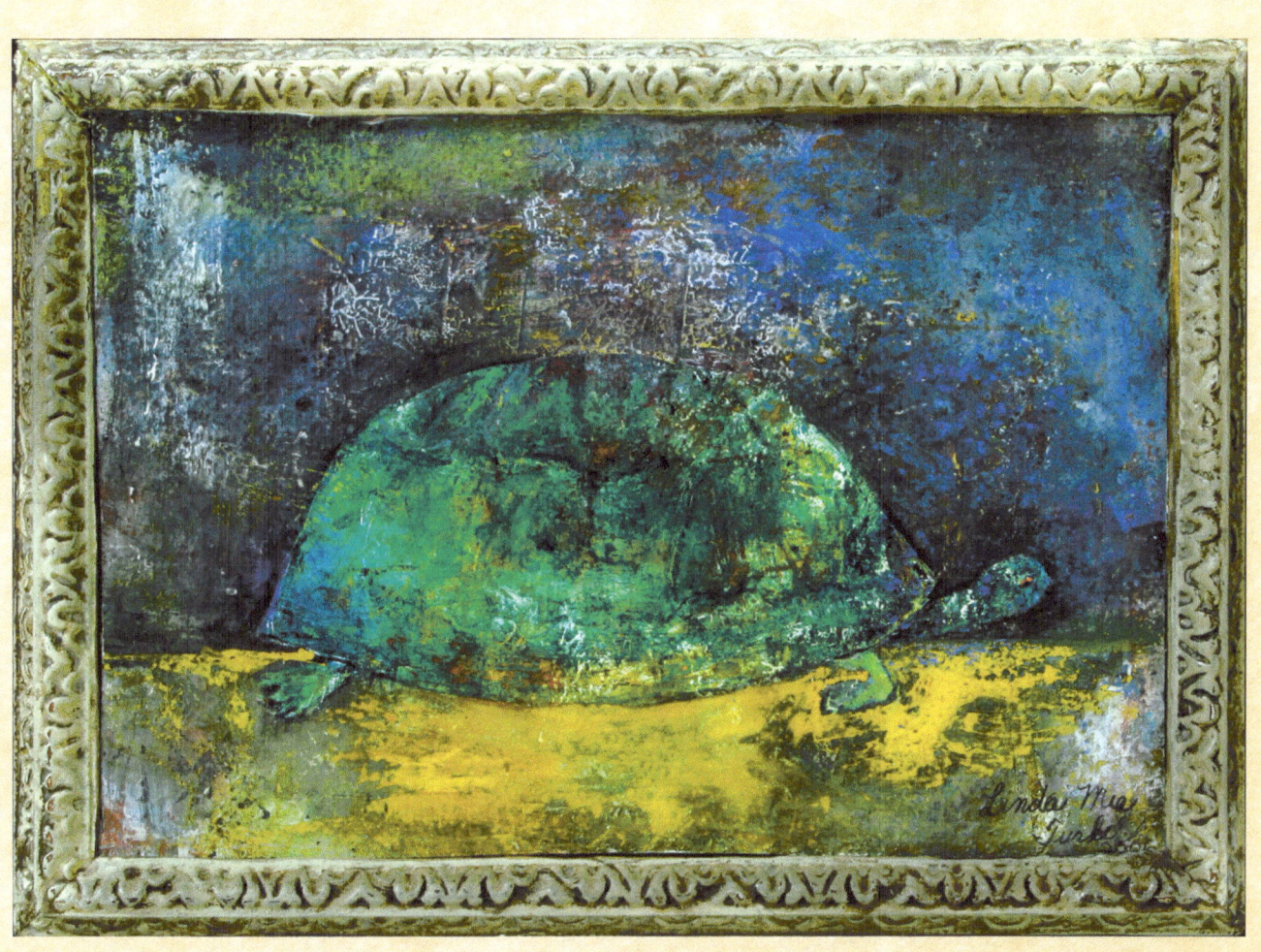

Upland Plover

I found this speckled bird

In the encyclopedia –

For I needed something starting with a "U."

He's protected by the government

Cause he eats harmful bugs.

And that is something

That I never knew.

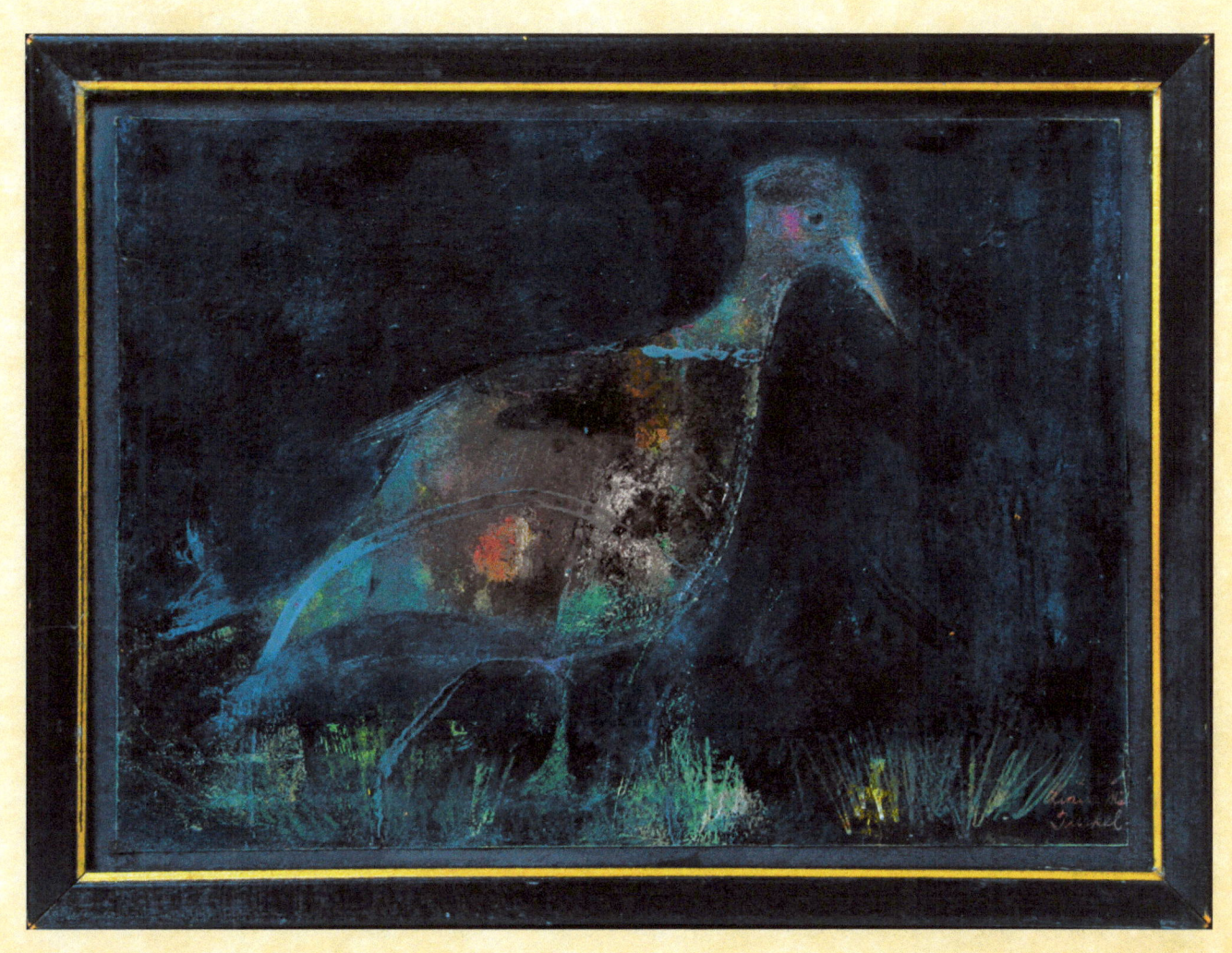

Vulture

The sharp eyes of the vulture

Can see for miles away.

He likes to eat his dinner

When it's started to decay.

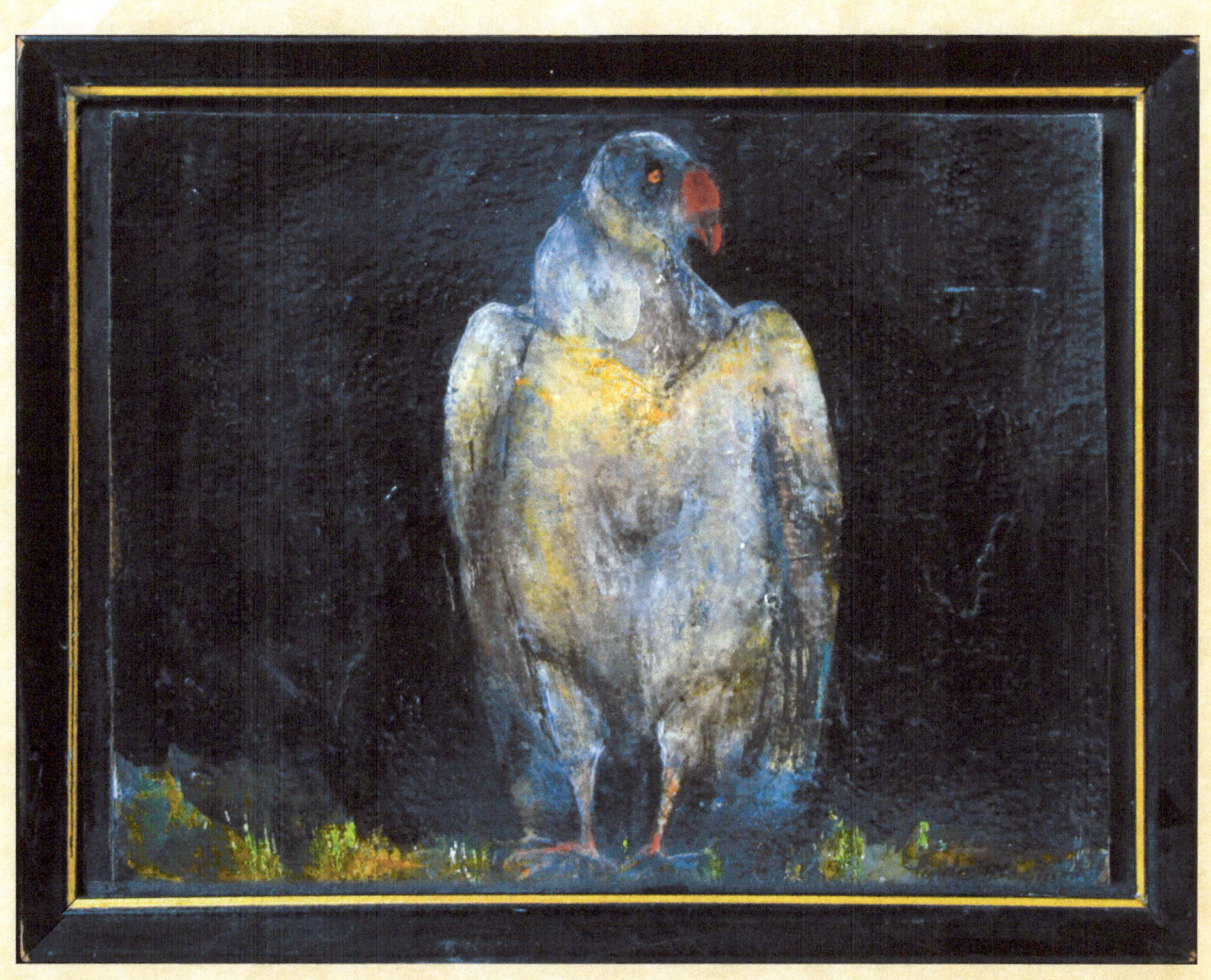

Wolf

He travels on the line

Between the wild and the tame.

And you can see the two things in his eyes.

He will answer to a person

Who has given him a name

And then you'll hear him

Howling at the skies.

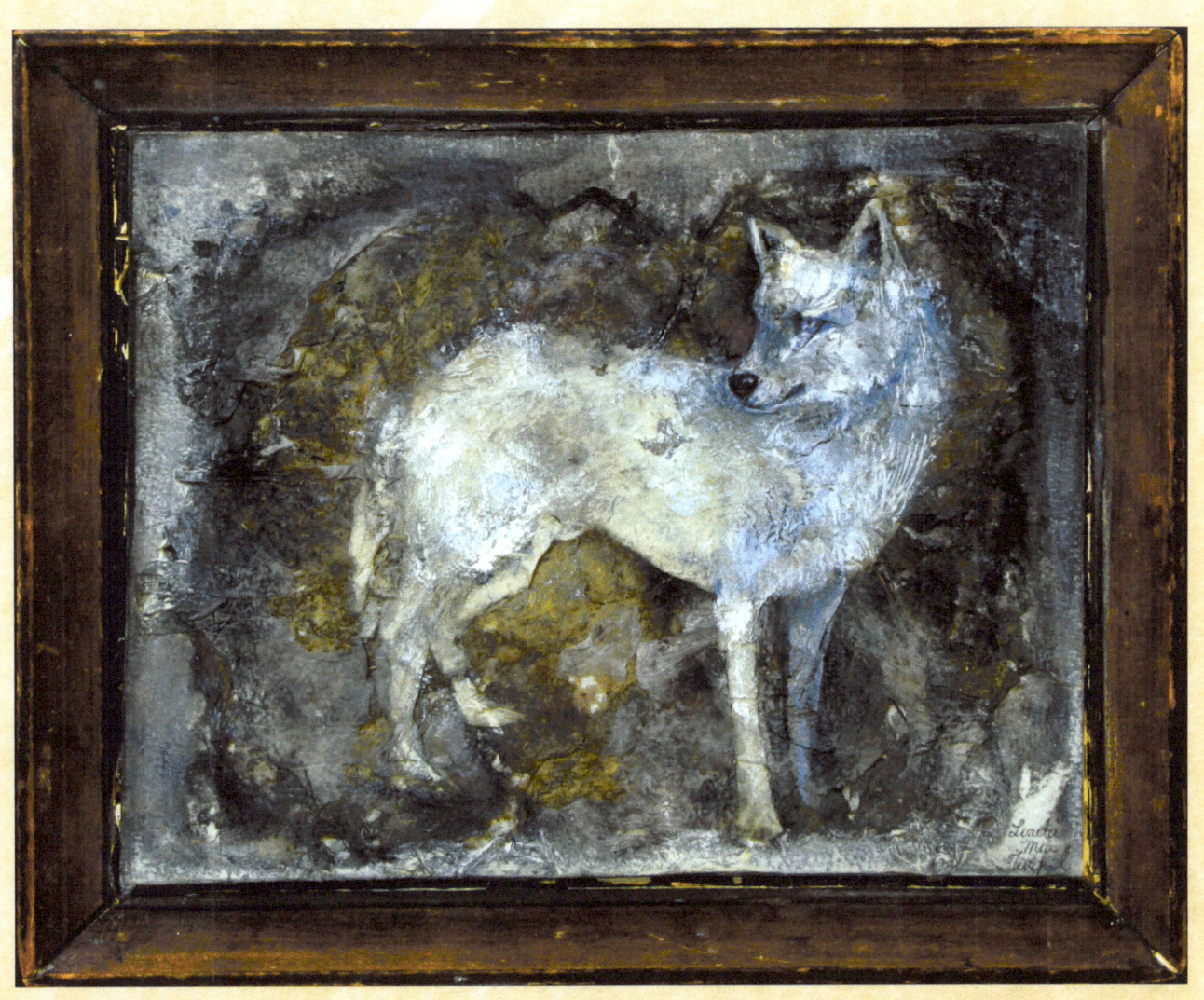

X-ray Fish

The x-ray fish is see-through.

It's a benefit alright!

For when it is pursued,

It can hide in plain sight.

47

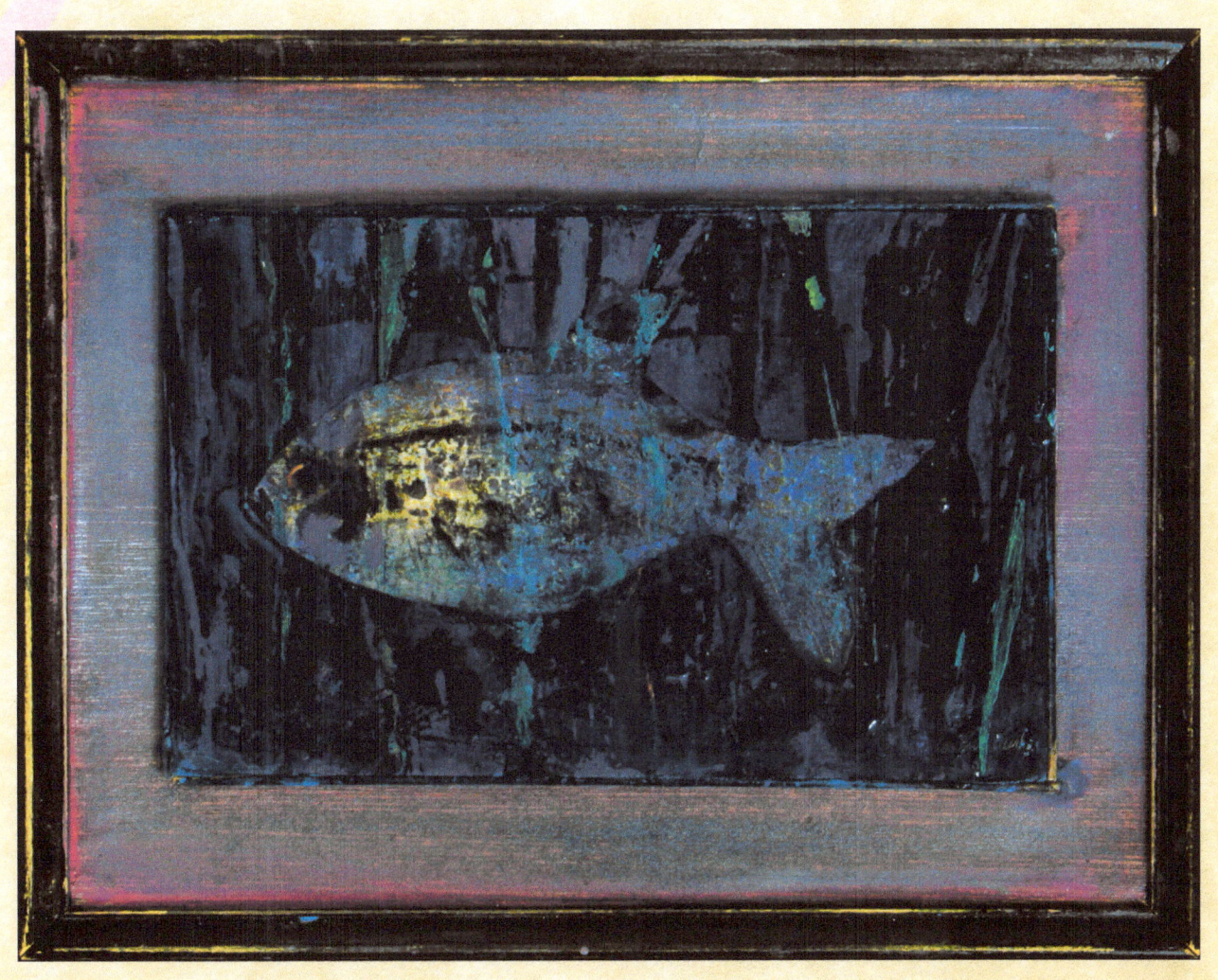

Yak

Up in the mountains of Tibet

Lives the shaggy yak.

He is a beast of burden

Yet if cornered will attack.

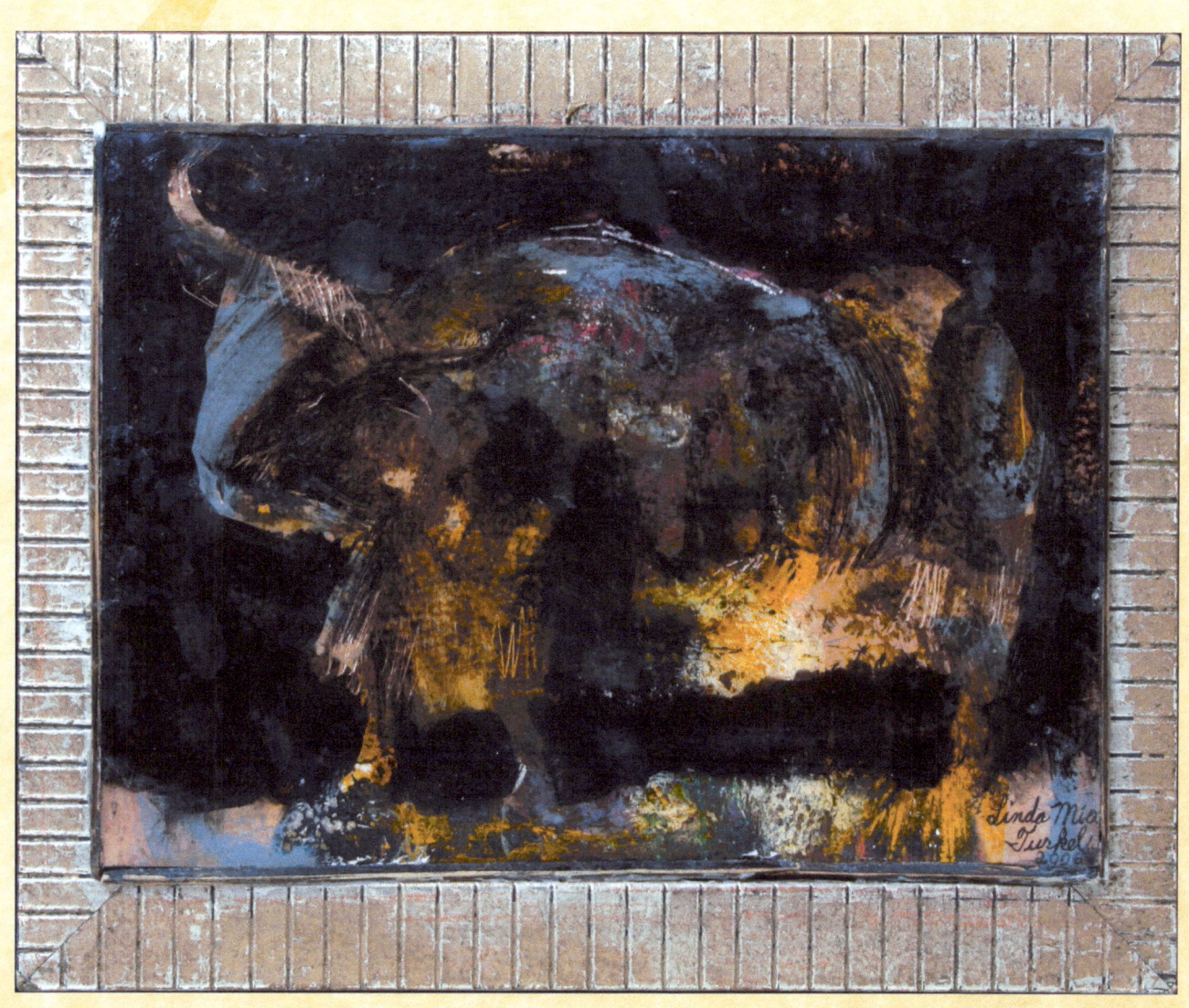

Zebra

The zebra's stripes wind 'round him

From his legs up to his mane.

And he does resemble

A liquorice candy cane.

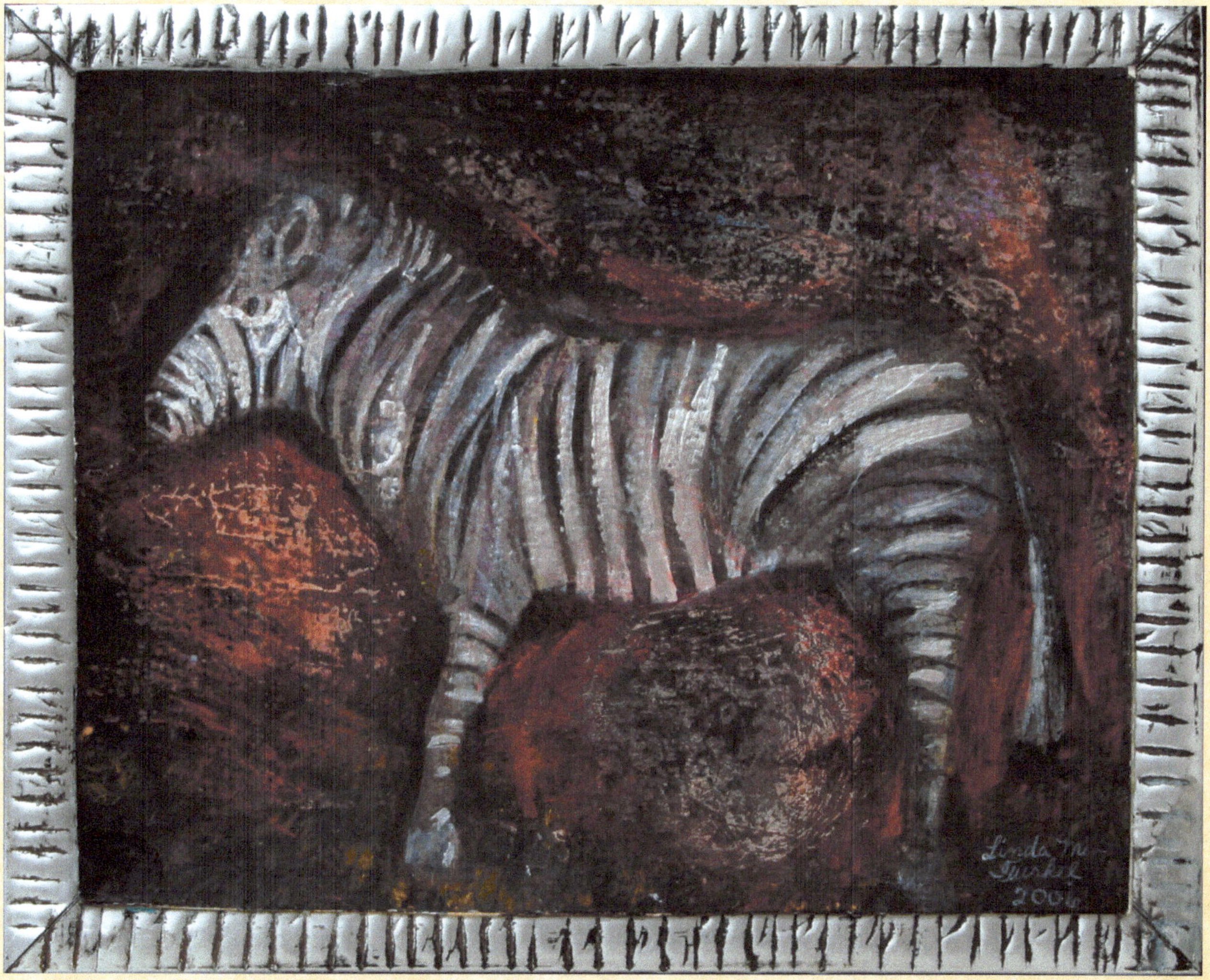

With special thanks to Dr. Inna Rozentsvit for her interest in publishing this book,
along with her prodigious efforts in making it all happen.

The END

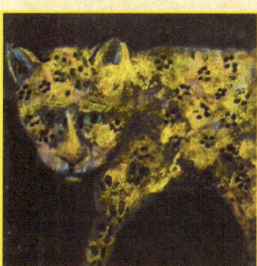

www.ingramcontent.com/pod-product-compliance
Lightning Source LLC
Chambersburg PA
CBHW050753180526
45159CB00003B/1444